W9-CMB-432

MAUI
A PICTURE MEMORY

Text
Bill Harris

Editorial
David Gibbon

Captions
Nicola Dent

Production
Ruth Arthur
Sally Connolly
Neil Randles
Andrew Whitelaw

Design
Teddy Hartshorn

Photography
Colour Library Books Ltd.
FPG International

Director of Production
Gerald Hughes

CLB 2868
© 1992 Colour Library Books Ltd., Godalming, Surrey, England
All rights reserved
This 1992 edition published by Crescent Books,
distributed by Outlet Book Company, Inc., a Random House Company,
40 Engelhard Avenue, Avenel, New Jersey 07001
Color separations by Scantrans Pte Ltd., Singapore
Printed and bound in Singapore
ISBN 0 517 07267 X
8 7 6 5 4 3 2 1

MAUI

A PICTURE MEMORY

CRESCENT BOOKS
NEW YORK • AVENEL, NEW JERSEY

First page: slender Iao Needle, western Maui, clad in emerald-green, lush vegetation, is one of Hawaii's finest volcanic wonders. Previous page: Maui's extensive beaches and rolling surf are excellent for water sports. Facing page: pleasure craft fill the harbor of historic Lahaina, former whaling capital of the Pacific.

When you're on vacation, the last thing you want to do is get up at the crack of dawn. But when the vacation is on the island of Maui, people routinely pop out of bed hours before dawn breaks, which happens between five-thirty and seven in the morning, depending on the season, and head for the hills.

More accurately, they head through the upcountry in the center of the island for the summit of Mount Haleakala. The road from sea level to the top of the 10,123-foot-high peak is only 38 miles long, but even rangers and others who work at Haleakala National Park and make the trip every day don't usually make it in much less than two hours. It is the only road in the world that climbs so high with so few switchbacks, and the drive is uphill most of the way. But if the going is slow, the destination is well worth it. The view from the Puu Ulaula Overlook includes the Big Island of Hawaii as well as Molokai, Kahoolawe and Lanai and, when it's clear, Oahu off to the northwest. But the best view first thing in the morning is toward the east, where the sun is about to make its appearance on the horizon.

Haleakala is the Hawaiian word for "House of the Sun," and it was from its summit, they say, that Maui himself captured and tamed the sun. According to the story, in ancient times the sun raced across the sky in such a hurry that days were much shorter than nights, which was a problem for women like Maui's mother, Hina, who depended on its warmth to dry the cloth called kapa, which they made from bark. After studying the problem, Maui noticed that the sun's daily path was directly over Haleakala, and one morning he went up to the top with a lasso. As the sun rushed by, he lashed out and snared one of its strongest beams. It slowed the sun's course a little but the beam broke and Maui was forced to lasso another, and then another, and yet another, until the sun finally agreed to listen to his proposition. Maui's demand was simple. All he asked was that the sun take it easy and linger longer over his island. It was better than losing all those rays and, from that day forward, the days on Maui's island were not only longer but sunnier. It was a great boon for kapa makers, wonderful for farmers, and terrific for vacationers.

The first *haole* – as Caucasians are known to the native islanders – to set foot on Maui was the English Captain James Cook, who anchored his ship there during his second visit to the islands in 1778. At the time the islands themselves were each ruled by a different king, and all of them were involved in what almost amounted to a constant state of war. Cook muddied the waters by inviting Kalaniopuu, the regent of the Big Island, to sail along the Maui shore with him. It was a direct insult to Maui's King Kahekili, but the two monarchs managed to ignore it. Kalaniopuu wasn't Cook's only native shipboard guest, however, among those in the king's retinue was his nephew, Kamehameha, a warrior with an ambition to be the only king of all the islands.

The old King Kalaniopuu had the same ambition, and not long after the English left, he sent 800 of his best warriors to take Maui by force, but they fell into a trap set for them by the wily Kahekili and only two survived the massacre that followed. Undaunted, the Hawaiian King sent a reserve force across the 65 miles of water that separates the two islands, but they, too, were wiped out, and Kalaniopuu not only lost the battles, but also the Hana coast which he had previously controlled.

It was Kalaniopuu's last battle. Not long after the fighting he proclaimed that his son, Kiwalao, would succeed him as king of the Big Island and that his nephew, Kamehameha, would be the earthly custodian of the war god of all the kings, Kukailimoku. This was a great honor for a young warrior, but not the one this particular warrior had in mind. When the king died, all the other kings went to war and Kiwalao was killed in one of the early battles. Kamehameha tried to take control, but Kahekili, the Maui chief, sided with another pretender and took advantage of the civil war that followed to spread his own kingdom to the island of Oahu.

Having acquired the island, Kahekili retired to the beach at Waikiki, leaving Maui open to attack. At the same time, Kamehameha had enlisted the help of two white adventurers, who supplied him with guns and the knowledge of how to use them, and before long he had conquered Molokai and Lanai as well as Maui. Soon after, he took control of Hawaii and Oahu and, a few years later, in 1810, he negotiated the allegiance of the island of Kauai, making him the first king of all the Hawaiian Islands. His capital city was Lahaina in West Maui.

Not long after Kamehameha I died, he was succeeded by his son, Liholiho, and one of his son's 21 wives, Kaahumanu, a Maui native who proclaimed herself Queen Regent. And that presented a problem. Since ancient times the islands have been subject to a system of inviolate kapus, known as taboos in other cultures. It was a pervasive set of rules that touched every Hawaiian, and anyone who broke one of them faced severe punishment, often death. Many of the kapus involved royalty. It was forbidden for the shadow of a commoner to touch a chief, for instance, and anyone in the presence of royalty was required to fall flat on the ground. Just as important were kapus that kept men and women separate. There were many foods, from bananas to pork, that were denied to women. And among the most important of all kapus was the rule that women and men should never eat at the same table together. Obviously, if a woman planned to share the rule of all the islands with a man, that custom needed to be changed.

It was easier said than done, but in 1819, at a state dinner in Kailua, King Liholiho changed everything. It's said that he had to spend two days sipping rum to work up the courage, but as he joined the guests at the banquet, he shocked everyone, possibly even himself, by sitting down at the table that had been set for the women. The following day he announced that the kapu system was henceforth abolished in all the islands, and his subjects, most of whom had grown up breaking the rules in secret, enthusiastically welcomed the idea. It made the Hawaiian Islands safe for the rule of a queen, but it was also a good omen for the passengers aboard a ship that had sailed for Hawaii from Boston a few days earlier.

Two of those passengers were Christian missionaries, the Reverend Hiram Bingham and the Reverend Asa Thurston, along with their wives, and accompanied by five other couples and the five children of one pair. Together they would change Hawaii more than any king had ever been able to do, and the inspiration that spurred them on was the abolition of kapus, which one of them said, "... is truly the Lord's doing and marvelous to our eyes."

The missionaries established their base at Honolulu, but they found their greatest challenge on Maui, where they considered the natives a good deal more heathenish than their neighbors. Another influence came in the shape of their own former neighbors, the crews of New England whaling ships who made Lahaina their most important port of call in the Pacific. In the mid 1820s a discouraged missionary summed up the problem he faced there when he wrote home that "the Devil is busily engaged in Lahaina as you may judge from the fact that 97 whale ships have anchored here." But the New Englander who received the letter may not have understood at all. Back home in Nantucket and New Bedford, the whale men generally behaved like Christians, but arriving after months at sea in a place where it was said hundreds of Hawaiian maidens regularly left their homes in the mountains to welcome the ships, even the most pious among them couldn't resist forgetting at least a couple of the Ten Commandments!

Even before the missionaries arrived, Yankee traders had done a booming business in sandalwood cut in the islands, and before nearly all the trees were destroyed many of the traders got rich. They shared some of the wealth with the local chiefs, and gave them a taste for such New England niceties as pool tables and beaver hats. But it was a haphazard business until a Massachusetts sailor named James Hunnewell agreed to transport the missionaries from island to island in exchange for the right to include a cargo of his own merchandise to sell to the Hawaiians. In four years he had made enough money to retire, but the company he founded stayed in business as C. Brewer & Co. to become the oldest of what is now known as "The Big Five," the American-oriented corporations that controlled the destiny of all the islands.

On Maui, sugar was king. Cane grew wild in all the islands and the missionaries turned cultivating it into a cottage industry, but it became big business when Samuel Alexander and Henry Baldwin, sons of missionaries, established plantations on Maui and formed the last of the Big Five companies, Alexander & Baldwin. What made the difference, beyond the fact that they didn't have the same soul-saving responsibilities as their fathers, was that the American Civil War had cut off domestic sugar in the Northern States and a whole new market was created for the Hawaiian product. Over the years, Alexander & Baldwin became the strongest entity on Maui and is still the island's biggest landowner.

Until quite recently, Alexander & Baldwin was the owner of the Wailea Resort on Maui's southwest coast that includes five picture-perfect, white, crescent beaches and Haleakala Crater in the background, which prevents rain and wind from spoiling long days of snorkeling and sunning. Wailea was developed in 1973, making it a relative newcomer to the general Hawaiian scene, but by Maui standards it's an old-timer. Tourism didn't arrive on Maui until the early 1960s, when the Amfac Corporation, another of the Big Five, opened the Kaanapali Beach Resort. It was the first resort in all of Hawaii to follow a master plan that made it a destination in itself, leaving the rest of the island relatively unspoiled. Wailea followed the same principle, and so did Kapalua, developed in the 1970s by Maui Land & Pineapple as one of the world's most luxurious resorts. There are other tourist destinations on the island, to be sure, but the three self-contained complexes keep Maui as natural and pristine as a vacation island can be, and although it welcomes more than two million visitors a year, there remain plenty of villages where the original Hawaiian language is still spoken, and places among the flowers that haven't changed since long before the original Polynesians arrived there.

The development of Maui as a tourist destination was by companies that all have a decidedly American accent. Both Maui Land & Pineapple and Alexander & Baldwin were founded by children of missionaries, but Amfac, even though its name is an acronym for American Factors, has a quite different history.

Through the years of the 19th century, Americans changed the ethnic mix of the Hawaiian Islands by encouraging Filipinos, Chinese and Japanese to augment the labor force. But English interests were at work, too, and exerted a strong influence on Hawaiian royalty, who regarded them as potential protectors against the Americans. Russians also tried hard to establish themselves, as did the Germans.

By the time World War I broke out in 1914, Hawaii had been a U.S. territory for 14 years, which made its harbors neutral territory, and German ships considered them safe havens. Under the rules of war, merchant ships could stay as long as they pleased, but warships were limited to a single day unless they were disabled. When a German gunboat appeared, it was allowed to stay pending repairs, but before her captain could put out to sea again, a Japanese battleship appeared on the horizon lying in wait. Rather than face a sure fight, the German allowed his ship to be impounded.

As the war dragged on, and it became more apparent that the U.S. would end its neutrality, anti-German feeling swept the islands and the people began worrying about the potential enemy seapower in their midst. The chief negotiator between the German and American governments was the head of the largest company in the islands, Hackfield & Company, and he also happened to be the German Consul. He was not only a tough negotiator, succeeding in resisting attempts to remove the crews from the gunboat and the other ships that were sitting out the war, but it was stated that he secured false passports that allowed the officers of the gunboat to slip away to the American mainland. His pro-German activities made it possible for the government to seize the company as enemy property, and by the time the war was over shares that had been owned by German nationals – nearly three-quarters of the outstanding stock – were resold to American businessmen. Hackfield & Company became American Factors Ltd., and although postwar lawsuits produced some compensation for the German entrepreneur who had founded the company, the Big Five was all-American from then on.

Tourism, which the sugar kings ignored through most of their early history, could almost have been considered an all-American affair from the beginning. Visitors began arriving in the middle of the 19th century, but only people with plenty of time and plenty of money could make the trip, even though as recently as a hundred years ago the round-trip fare from San Francisco was only $125. The early guidebooks concentrated on Oahu and the Big Island, and the others were left to the imagination of adventuresome tourists, who largely passed Maui by.

Such a fact boggles the imagination today, now that Maui has become the second most-visited of all the Hawaiian Islands. It amazes the Hawaiians themselves, because as recently as a generation ago it would have been inconceivable that half the population should earn its living from tourism, or that Maui would be home to more millionaires per capita than any other corner of the United States. It amazes them, but it doesn't surprise anyone else. It is hard to imagine a more beautiful tropical island, even among the 132 islands and atolls that surround it.

Like many of the other islands, Maui was created by volcanoes. The older of the two is the 5,788-foot-high Puu Kukui in West Maui, which is now extinct, and the other is the spectacular Haleakala, the biggest dormant volcano in the world. Ancient eruptions from both joined them into a single island, with a lush valley between them that gives Maui its other name, "the Valley Isle." The two mountains could hardly be called twins, for Puu Kukui is famed for its rainbows and its bigger companion is hidden in clouds much of the time. But their legacy is rich, red soil that contrasts with the green of sugar cane and the endless colors of tropical flowers, and complements the deep blue of the sea and sky and the fleecy-white clouds overhead.

Because of the careful planning that went into its resorts, Maui isn't quite the sightseeing destination that its natural beauty suggests. But for combining gorgeous scenery with pure adventure, nothing in the world compares with a drive on the Hana Highway, a 53-mile-long trip from the Kahului Airport to the town of Hana along the island's northeast coast. It's a serpentine affair, with some 617 sharp turns and 56 one-lane bridges hacked out along the coastline. But there are plenty of places to stop, where you can unlock your hands from the steering wheel and either relax your fingers in the spray from a towering waterfall or by stroking the velvety fronds of a tropical fern. There are jungle trails to explore and scenic overlooks to take your breath away, and all along the way flowering plants fight for attention. It is one of the most popular drives in all of the islands in spite of its harrowing turns, or perhaps for some, because of them. But it is only one of Maui's special delights.

Where else can you sleep in an ultra-modern hotel, with every convenience imaginable, get in a round of golf, lie on a pristine beach, visit an authentic 19th-century whaling village, watch a family of humpback whales and visit a cattle ranch all in the same day? And if you haven't eaten a Maui onion, crunched one of the island's own versions of the potato chip, or sampled wine made from grapes grown on Haleakala's slopes, you've missed some of Hawaii's greatest pleasures. And speaking of Haleakala, almost no one who has ever driven up to the summit hasn't thought of what it must be like to be riding a bicycle along that same road. It is obviously more fun coming down than going up, and the ever-accommodating Mauians have made it possible by providing a service that takes passengers up the mountain in a van and lets them coast back down by bicycle without the need to touch the pedals anywhere on the 38-mile run, which they call a cruise. The trip includes stops for lunch and usually ends with a dinner. In between are spectacular views of cattle ranches, cane fields and forests of protea, a transplanted South African flower that comes in an almost endless variety of sizes and colors and, on Maui at least, has become a bigger cash crop than either orchids or the protea's second cousin, macadamia nuts.

The bike ride is not your average cruise, to be sure, but then Maui is not your average tropical paradise. Its wide diversity of landscapes, that include the awe-inspiring Haleakala National Park and miles of unspoiled beaches and rocky coastline, the island's remarkable tropical flora and fauna, its luxurious hotel resorts and its friendly people, all combine to make a visit to Maui a magical and memorable experience.

Verdant Iao Valley (facing page), near Wailuku, encompasses the dormant crater area of West Maui. This is the smaller of the two volcanic peaks that fused together thousands of years ago to form the island of Maui, and is joined to East Maui by a narrow strip of land. This isthmus has given Maui its nickname, "the Valley Isle."

These pages: some of Maui's most stunning and varied views can be seen from the Hana Highway, which winds along the northern coast for over 50 miles towards Hana. The jagged lava shore of the Keanae Peninsula, washed by the Pacific surf, contrasts with patchwork-like fields of taro (facing page bottom and overleaf), a starchy rootcrop pounded to produce poi, once a Hawaiian staple food. Below: Haipuaena Falls, near Keanae, one of several scenic cascades seen en route to Hana.

The tropical climate of Hawaii supports many vibrant blooms, and the range of color, shape and species is stunning. Among the various flowers are giant red and yellow heliconia (above), delicate plumeria or frangipani (top right and facing page top), Hawaii's national flower: the hibiscus (right), cassia alata (bottom right), rocket protea (below), and ixora (facing page bottom), a relative of the coffee plant. Overleaf: red anthuriums thrive in the shelter of tree ferns.

Waianapanapa State Park (these pages), a seaside area in East Maui, three miles from Hana, is known for its rugged scenery which includes a natural rock arch (bottom right), two water-filled lava tubes, and dramatic Honokalani Beach (facing page top) at Pailoa Bay, one of the few black beaches on Maui. The area is surrounded by tropical vegetation dotted with delicate Queen Emma lilies (facing page bottom) and other flowers. Overleaf: a stretch of lava coastline near Hana.

East Maui's unique Oheo Gulch or Seven "Sacred" Pools (above, left and overleaf), are one of the main attractions in the coastal section of Haleakala National Park. A favorite with visitors for swimming and picnicking, the area is renowned for its seven large pools and several smaller pools, through which fresh water cascades down to the sea. Facing page: nearby Wailua Falls tumble amid tropical plants, and (remaining pictures) the rocky coastline close to Seven Pools.

Haleakala National Park (these pages) was established in 1961 to preserve the remarkable Haleakala Crater. Part of the largest dormant volcano in the world, the crater is known by Hawaiians as the "House of the Sun," after a legend in which the demigod Maui captured the sun in order to persuade it to move more slowly across the sky each day. The rare silversword (left), thought to be unique to this area, and yellow poppies (facing page bottom), provide a welcome splash of color to the lunar-like landscape. Below: evidence of past volcanic activity shown by old cinder cones, and (overleaf) a dramatic view from the summit of the volcano.

Maui's most visited attraction, Haleakala National Park is dominated
by the towering, 10,023-foot-high summit of Mount Haleakala. Despite
its great altitude the area is popular with hikers, explorers and scientists,
and the Park Service has provided three rustic cabins and a visitors'
center (below) within the crater. Calculated to be vast enough to house
Manhattan Island, dramatic vistas and fine sunsets (remaining pictures
and overleaf) are part of the splendor and appeal of this national park.

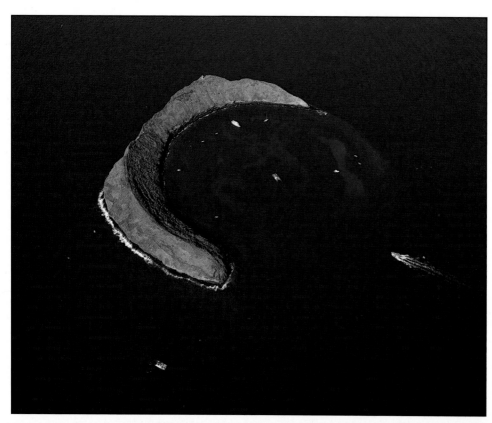

Left: tiny, crescent-shaped Molokini Island, off the west coast of Maui, is comprised of the remains of a volcanic cinder cone. Particularly known for the superb snorkelling, scuba and skin-diving it offers, traditional Hawaiians still respect the island as the home of ancestral spirits. Below: an aerial view of the western coast of East Maui, near Kihei. Facing page: sunset seen from Haleakala Highway (top), and views westwards from Highway 377 (bottom) looking towards the cloud-covered West Maui Mountains.

One of the attractions of the Hawaiian Islands is the remarkable profusion of flora, in particular the vivid, multi-hued flowers. These are often used to decorate drinks, for export, and for making "leis," the traditional garland for greeting visitors. Right: bourgainvillea, and (center right) fragrant plumeria, the main bloom used in leis. Below: a bird of paradise flower, and (bottom right) one of Maui's exotic gardens.

Iao Needle (top left and facing page), with the Iao Stream in the foreground, is the site where King Kamehameha I defeated the Maui army in 1790. The stream was so choked with bodies that the area was named Kepaniwai, meaning "the damming of the waters." Nearby are the Kepaniwai Heritage Gardens (left, bottom left and overleaf), filled with pavilions and ornamental gardens that reflect various cultures of ethnic groups in Maui, for example the Japanese Heritage Garden (below). Above: a roadside shrine.

Lahaina (these pages and overleaf), once a busy whaling port, has kept much of the charm and architecture of its past. Notable features include the restored 1901 Pioneer Inn (right), now full of whaling artifacts, Carthaginian II (facing page top), a replica of a typical whaling ship, and Victorian-style Lahaina Station, home to the 1890s Sugar Cane Train (facing page bottom). North of the town is the Japanese Cultural Park of the Lahaina Jodo Mission, famed for its giant bronze Buddha (above).

Lahaina's extensive conservation program and the town's increasing popularity have led to a unique blend of past and present. Left: the balconied Pioneer Inn, West Maui's only lodgings for visitors until the late 1950s, contrasts with a luxury beachside hotel (center left). Remaining pictures and overleaf: Lahaina's picturesque harbor with its fine backdrop of gently-contoured West Maui Mountains.

Set in eight acres of land in southern Kaanapali, near Lahaini, Whaler's Village and Museum (top right) is an unusual shopping complex containing restaurants, a cinema, land-scaped gardens and an amphitheater. The area also features a whaling museum with a 40-foot-long sperm whale skeleton (right) as the focal point of its exhibits. Remaining pictures and overleaf: an attractive golden beach close to Whaler's Village, with the island of Lanai seen in the distance.

Maui's West Coast is particularly attractive to tourists, with its many beach resorts, excellent hotels, and stunning scenery. The magnificent golden Kaanapali Beach Resort (facing page) is home to some of Hawaii's finest and most luxurious hotels including the Hyatt Regency Maui (top left) and the Royal Lahaina Hotel (bottom left). Left: one of the famed golf courses that is among the resort's excellent facilities. Above and below: sailing craft silhouetted against a sunset at Wahikuli State Park.

Expanses of sugar cane (right), seen from Honoapiilani Highway, and fields of glossy, green pineapple plants (top right and over-leaf), are examples of the crops that were once the major source of Maui's income. Mokuleia Bay (above), Kahana Beach (facing page top) and, further south, Wahikuli State Park (facing page bottom), show signs of the more recent tourist industry which has rapidly overtaken the declining agricultural trade. Below: Kapalua Bay and (bottom right) Nakalele Point, West Maui.

The Hawaii Islands are renowned for their world-class surfing, known in Hawaiian as "heenalu" or wave sliding, and are the venue for many international championships. Surfers are seen here riding the Pacific waves at Honolua Bay (these pages), West Maui. South of this inlet is Kaanapali (overleaf), a three-mile-long beach, particularly famous for the splendor of its sunsets. Last page: a typical, but unforgettable Hawaiian scene – a palm silhouetted against a deep-orange sunset.